A BUSINESS APPROACH TO ORCHID FARMING

I0430023

Complete Entrepreneurial Step By Step Guide To Orchid Garden From Scratch

ZHURI HART

DISCLAIMER

This book is intended to provide general information and insights on adopting a business approach to farming. The content within is based on the author's knowledge and experiences up to the date of publication. It is essential to recognize that the field of agriculture is dynamic, influenced by various factors such as market conditions, climate, and regulatory changes.

Readers are advised to conduct thorough research, seek professional advice, and consider their unique circumstances before implementing any strategies or practices discussed in this book. The author and publisher disclaim any responsibility for the accuracy, completeness, or suitability of the information provided. The book is not a substitute for professional advice, and the author and publisher shall not be liable for any damages or losses arising from the use or reliance on the information presented herein.

Individual results may vary, and success in farming enterprises is contingent upon numerous variables. The author encourages readers to consult with relevant experts, agricultural extension services, and legal or financial professionals to tailor strategies to their specific needs and local conditions.

This book is not intended to be a comprehensive guide to all aspects of farming, and readers should exercise their judgment and discretion in applying the principles discussed. The author and publisher do not endorse any specific products, services, or companies mentioned in this book unless explicitly stated.

By reading this book, the reader acknowledges and accepts the inherent uncertainties in agricultural endeavors and agrees to use the information at their own risk.

TABLE OF CONTENTS

ABOUT THE BOOK

"A Business Approach to Orchid Farming" is a thorough manual that explores the complex world of orchid growing and offers a tactical foundation to anyone hoping to launch a profitable orchid farming business. Because of the market's great importance and the variety of orchid species that exist, this book is a great tool for both amateurs and business owners.

The book opens with a perceptive introduction that highlights the wider significance of orchids in the market and provides an outline of orchid farming. It lays forth specific goals, making it easier for readers to comprehend the book's scope and intent.

The core of the book is the Understanding Orchids section, which explores the varieties, traits, and environments in which orchids develop. Anyone hoping to get into orchid growing needs to know this information. Equally important is the part on orchid propagation techniques, which offers comprehensive information on a range of techniques like hybridization, tissue culture, division, and seed propagation.

The practical side of the company is covered in Setting Up Your Orchid Farm, which includes choosing a good location, designing the greenhouse, and acquiring the required tools. Orchid Business Planning, walks readers through creating a strong business strategy, conducting market research, developing pricing strategies, and setting up channels for sales and distribution. The book inclusion of financial management elements adds a critical layer by highlighting the significance of funding acquisition, cost analysis, and budgeting.

In addition, the book guides readers through the complex world of orchid care and maintenance while providing insightful advice on pest control, soil combinations, and watering techniques. Key insights into recognizing profitable varieties, comprehending market trends, and developing successful branding and marketing strategies may be found in the chapters on

Orchid Species and Cultivars for Profitability and Marketing Your Orchids.

 The book also discusses issues related to orchid growing and offers creative solutions, enabling readers to overcome any roadblocks. Future Trends in Orchid Farming offers a forward-looking viewpoint by projecting global market trends, sustainable practices, and developing technologies.

"A Business Approach to Orchid Farming" is essentially a strategy guidebook that provides readers with the information and resources they need to succeed in the exciting and lucrative world of orchid farming, rather than merely a manual. This book is a priceless tool for anyone looking to succeed in the orchid farming industry, regardless of level of expertise.

CHAPTER ONE

ORCHID FARMING INTRODUCTION
AN OVERVIEW OF GROWING ORCHIDS

The commercial cultivation of orchidaceous plants is known as orchid farming, and it has become a prominent and separate industry within the larger field of horticulture. This elaborate procedure entails the methodical raising of orchids, which are prized for their varied and appealing bouquets.

With a wide range of species, hybrids, and variants, orchids are among the largest and most diverse families of flowering plants. Orchid farming is the application of many approaches, ranging from sophisticated greenhouse technologies to traditional ways, to meet the unique needs of numerous orchid species.

The economic significance of orchids adds to their charm in addition to their visual appeal. Because of their beautiful appeal, orchids have a special place in the market and are highly sought after for a variety of uses. Orchids are popular in flower arrangements, decorative displays, and landscaping projects because of their diversity, which guarantees a wide choice of colors, forms, and sizes.

Furthermore, the growing admiration for these exotic blooms in both local and foreign markets has led to a steady increase in the demand for orchids worldwide.

ORCHIDS' SIGNIFICANCE IN THE MARKET

Orchids are important to the market for reasons other than just aesthetics. Orchids are essential to several businesses, such as pharmaceuticals, perfumery, and floristry. Some orchid species are valuable ingredients in perfume manufacture because of their distinct scents, which provide the fragrance industry with a distinctive and exotic touch.

In addition, the medical qualities of some orchids have drawn attention from the pharmaceutical industry, and studies investigating their possible therapeutic uses are currently underway.

Orchids have an important commercial role, but they also greatly enhance biodiversity and ecological balance.

Due to habitat degradation and overexploitation, many orchid species are endangered or at risk, hence conservation efforts are frequently incorporated into orchid farming operations.

To meet market demands and preserve the natural habitats of these attractive flowers, sustainable orchid farming practices are combined with conservation measures.

Orchid farming is a complex and diverse endeavor that entails more than just the production of exquisite blossoms. The attraction of orchids has created a unique market niche, impacting several sectors and encouraging a careful balancing act between profit and environmental preservation.

It becomes clear as we look more into the complex world of orchid production that these beautiful blossoms are more than simply commodities—they are symbols of beauty, cultural value, and ecological worth.

CHAPTER TWO

KNOWING ABOUT ORCHIDS

ORCHID TYPES

As members of the Orchidaceae family, one of the biggest families of flowering plants, orchids are a varied and intriguing group of blooming plants. Orchids come in an amazing variety of forms, sizes, and colors, with over 25,000 species and over 100,000 hybrids. Orchid classification is determined by several variables, such as flower form, growth behaviors, and root system composition. The Phalaenopsis, Cattleya, Dendrobium, Oncidium, and Vanda are a few common orchid species; each has unique traits and needs.

WELL-LIKED TYPES

Of the many orchid variants, some species and hybrids have become very popular with collectors and enthusiasts. The Phalaenopsis orchid, also called the "moth orchid," is a widely grown kind distinguished by its gracefully curved stems and vivid blossoms. For orchid fans, cattleya orchids are a favorite as well, due to their enormous, spectacular blossoms and intriguing aroma. In addition, the Miltoniopsis, or pansy orchid, is a popular choice due to its delicate and delicately patterned blossoms. Different orchid kinds are more or less popular depending on things like care requirements, visual attractiveness, and distinctive features.

FEATURES AND GROWING ENVIRONMENT

With their ability to adapt to a wide range of conditions worldwide, orchids display an amazing assortment of features. Their special method of reproduction, which involves complex interactions with pollinators like bees, butterflies, and moths, is one of their distinguishing characteristics. Orchids can be terrestrial, living in the soil, or epiphytic, growing on trees and getting their nourishment from the rain and air. Aerial roots and pseudobulbs are examples of specialized structures found in most orchids, which aid in their adaptability. Although growing conditions for orchids differ depending on the species, they usually include a well-draining orchid mix, suitable humidity levels, and the right amount of sun exposure. In general, orchids need a careful mix of care, which includes accurate fertilization, temperature control, and watering.

LIFE CYCLE OF ORCHIDS

An orchid's life cycle is an intriguing trip with various stages. As tiny seeds, orchids frequently depend on fungi to germinate. The seed that germinates grows into a protocorm, which then becomes a fully-grown plant. The development of roots and leaves during the growth stage results in the maturation of the orchid. The ability of orchids to make extremely specialized flowers is well known, and it is essential to their reproductive process. The orchid life cycle is ensured by its complex dance with pollinators. After pollination, orchids generate seed pods that house hundreds of tiny seeds, which scatter and locate ideal places for germination to complete the cycle.

ENVIRONMENTAL ELEMENTS THAT IMPACT ORCHID DEVELOPMENT

Orchid cultivation success mostly depends on knowing and controlling environmental elements that affect the plants' growth. Both the time and the intensity of the light are important; many orchids prefer dappled or filtered light over direct sunshine. Orchid growth is influenced by seasonal and diurnal temperature fluctuations since different species have preferred temperatures. The majority of orchids grow best in situations with moderate to high humidity, thus humidity levels are also essential. For healthy growth and the prevention of fungal diseases, proper air circulation is crucial. The choices of growing media and water quality also have a big impact on orchid health. Orchids are a rewarding and complex addition to the world of gardening, but growing them requires balancing several environmental elements.

CHAPTER THREE

ESTABLISHING AN ORCHID FARM

CHOOSING AN APPROPRIATE LOCATION

The careful selection of a suitable location is a critical component of an orchid farm's success. Particular environmental factors, such as temperature, humidity, and light, are favorable to orchid growth. As such, picking a location that provides ideal growing circumstances for the particular orchid kinds you want to grow is essential. It is necessary to take into account variables like altitude, climate, and distance from water sources. A setting that offers a balance between sunlight and shade is ideal, as orchid growth can be negatively impacted by extended exposure to bright sunlight or extreme shadow.

DESIGN AND CONSTRUCTION OF GREENHOUSES

Any orchid farm would not be complete without a greenhouse, which offers a regulated climate ideal for orchid development. The greenhouse's layout and construction are essential to establishing the ideal environment for orchid growth. It is important to take into account elements like temperature regulation, ventilation, and the usage of shade materials. The greenhouse's construction needs to be easily maintained accessible, and robust enough to survive environmental obstacles. To fully utilize the greenhouse, effective watering systems and benches designed specifically for orchid development and display must be included.

ESSENTIAL INSTRUMENTS AND EQUIPMENT

Having the appropriate tools and equipment for your orchid farm is essential to effective and productive growing. Pruning shears, misting systems, humidity meters, and temperature controllers are a few examples of essential tools. Purchasing top-notch tools guarantees orchid care with accuracy and improves the plants' general health. Sufficient pest management strategies, like using insecticides or utilizing advantageous predators, have to be contemplated to safeguard orchids against possible hazards. Long-term production on the farm depends on regular maintenance of the tools and machinery.

ORCHID FARM DESIGN AND LAYOUT

An orchid farm's layout is an important strategic factor that affects both the facility's overall aesthetic appeal and the effectiveness of its operation. A well-planned project should take accessibility, space needs, and the kind of orchids being grown into consideration. To enable focused care, orchids that require different amounts of light and temperature should be put together appropriately. Walkways and paths should be made for easy maintenance and navigation. An orderly and visually pleasant arrangement of the benches, display places, and working spaces is a result of careful positioning. Scalability and adaptation to future modifications in cultivation techniques or the introduction of new orchid types are made possible by the layout design's flexibility.

Careful consideration of site selection, greenhouse design, equipment acquisition, and layout planning is essential for the successful construction of an orchid farm. Orchid enthusiasts may build a successful and sustainable environment for raising these magnificent plants by taking into account these fundamentals.

CHAPTER FOUR

PROFITABLE ORCHID SPECIES AND CULTIVARS

FINDING COMMERCIALLY SUCCESSFUL ORCHID VARIETIES

Finding the orchid varieties with the highest potential for financial success is an essential first step in the profitable cultivation of orchids. This calls for a sophisticated comprehension of consumer demand in addition to an acute awareness of the distinguishing characteristics that set one orchid species or cultivar apart from another. The market value of an orchid is heavily influenced by variables including bloom size, color variations, and distinctive scents. A particular orchid variety's resilience and adaptability must also be taken into account for successful cultivation and long-term financial gain. To determine which orchid types are more popular than others, growers frequently carry out market research and interact with local and international orchid aficionados.

This information helps them decide which orchids should be prioritized for production.

CONSUMER PREFERENCES AND MARKET TRENDS

Orchid growers hoping to make a profit must remain aware of market developments and comprehend consumer preferences. The market for orchids is ever-changing due to changes in consumer preferences, fashion trends, and environmental awareness. Growers can better coordinate their cultivation efforts with changing consumer needs by staying updated on these changes. In the market, ornamental types, unusual hybrids, or orchids with particular cultural value are frequently sought after. Additionally, people who care about the environment find it appealing to use sustainable and eco-friendly procedures. Growers can gain important insights into new trends and shifting consumer tastes by regularly attending industry events, taking part in orchid exhibits, and utilizing internet platforms. This will help them position their orchids strategically in the market.

SPECIALIZED METHODS FOR GROWING ORCHIDS

Profitable orchid production frequently requires the use of specialized methods designed to meet the particular needs of each kind of orchid. The dietary requirements, growth patterns, and environmental preferences of orchids vary widely. Therefore, it is imperative to utilize particular growing procedures to maximize growth and guarantee the quality of the blooms. Methods like controlled environment agriculture (CEA), which include precisely regulating elements like light, humidity, and temperature, can be crucial to producing high-quality and reliable orchid yields. Additionally, by using cutting-edge propagation techniques like hybridization and tissue culture, farmers may produce orchids with desired characteristics, giving them a competitive advantage in the market. In addition to improving the general health of the orchids, sustainable production techniques like integrated pest management and organic fertilization also meet consumer demand for green products.

Growing orchids for profit necessitates a comprehensive strategy that includes identifying profitable types, keeping a close eye on market trends, and utilizing specialized cultivation techniques. Orchid producers may effectively navigate the complex market landscape and meet consumer expectations while maintaining sustainable and profitable methods by combining these components.

CHAPTER FIVE

METHODS OF PROPAGATING ORCHIDS

PROPAGATION OF SEEDS

One popular and organic way to reproduce orchids is by seed propagation. Unlike most plant seeds, orchid seeds are small and resemble dust; they do not include endosperm. As a result, for germination, they need a symbiotic interaction with fungi. Orchid seeds need a particular kind of fungus to colonize their surface and supply vital nutrients for growth since they are frequently distributed through the air.

Gathering mature seed pods, sterilizing them, and then planting the seeds onto an appropriate medium—such as agar—are the steps involved in the process of propagating seeds. Because orchid seeds are sensitive, this method makes it possible to produce a huge number of orchids, but it also necessitates careful attention to environmental conditions and aseptic techniques.

PARTITION AND REDUCTIONS

Common vegetative growth techniques for orchids with rhizomes or pseudobulbs are division and offsets. Pseudobulbs are organs of storage that hold water and nutrients, enabling orchids to endure harsh environments. A mature orchid plant is divided into two or more pieces, each having a rhizome or pseudobulb of its own. Little plantlets called offsets, or keikis, grow at the base of the mother plant or along its stem. It is possible to separate these offsets and grow them into separate plants. When propagating orchids, especially those with well-developed pseudobulbs, division, and offsets are both efficient methods that allow for faster reproduction than seed propagation.

METHODS FOR TISSUE CULTURE

Tissue culture techniques, which provide a more controlled and effective means of mass-producing orchids, are becoming more and more common in the propagation of orchids. Isolating and growing individual cells or tissues in a sterile setting are the process of tissue culture. A little piece of tissue, frequently removed from the pseudobulb or shoot tip, is inserted into a nutrient-rich solution during orchid propagation to promote the growth of new roots and shoots. With this technique, a lot of genetically identical orchids can be produced in a short amount of time. When it comes to maintaining and propagating uncommon or endangered orchid species, tissue culture is quite helpful.

HYBRIDIZATION TO PROVIDE SPECIAL VARIETIES

One method used to produce distinctive orchid varieties with desirable features is hybridization.

Crossbreeding two distinct orchid species or variations results in offspring that combine the traits of both parents. This process is known as orchid hybridization. Hand pollination is a common method used to carry out this operation, in which the stigma of one orchid is pollinated by hand. Growers and breeders may give orchids new colors, forms, and scents through hybridization. The resultant hybrids might be more vigorous, resistant to disease, or able to adapt to certain growth environments. The diversity and beauty of cultivated orchids around the world are largely due to hybridization, which is essential to the creation of new orchid varieties.

CHAPTER SIX

MAINTENANCE AND CARE FOR ORCHIDS

SOIL AND POTTING COMBINATIONS

It is well known that orchids have specific needs in terms of soil and potting combinations. Orchids, in contrast to many other plants, are usually epiphytic— that is, they grow on surfaces other than soil. Those who are passionate about orchids frequently use specialty potting mixes that replicate the loose, well-draining conditions that orchids like. Bark, coconut husk pieces, sphagnum moss, and perlite are frequent ingredients in orchid mixes.

This mixture ensures appropriate oxygen exchange and prevents waterlogging by encouraging aeration around the roots of the orchid. Because orchids have different tastes, it's important to know what each variety of orchid requires to cultivate them successfully.

WATERING AND HUMIDITY MANAGEMENT

Proper watering is essential for orchid maintenance. While underwatering may cause dehydration, overwatering might cause root rot. In general, orchids want a period of drying out in between watering to avoid having their roots remain moist all the time. The type of orchid being grown, the potting material being used, and the surrounding conditions all affect how frequently an orchid has to be watered. Orchids also require appropriate humidity maintenance because they frequently flourish in humid areas. Techniques like utilizing a humidifier or setting up water trays next to orchids can assist in achieving the appropriate moisture levels. To maintain a healthy moisture balance and avoid fungal problems and stagnant air, adequate ventilation is crucial.

FERTILIZATION PROCEDURES

Since orchids typically thrive in nutrient-poor settings in their native habitats, fertilization is an essential part of orchid maintenance. It's usual practice to utilize specialized orchid fertilizers that have balanced ratios of trace elements, phosphorus, potassium, and nitrogen. The type of orchid and the growing media affect how frequently they are fertilized. In spring and summer, orchids are in their active growing season and may benefit from fertilizer more frequently. Nonetheless, it's normally advised to cut back on or stop feeding during the dormant season, which occurs in the fall and winter. It's important to follow the directions on the packet to prevent overfertilizing, which could damage the orchids.

PEST AND DISEASE MANAGEMENT

Because orchids are vulnerable to a wide range of pests and diseases, it is crucial to keep a close eye on them to identify problems early and take appropriate action. Aphids, spider mites, and scale insects are common pests. Control can be achieved by using natural predators such as beneficial insects or insecticidal soaps.

A healthy atmosphere can be preserved with the help of preventive actions like routinely checking the foliage and cleaning the growth space. Additionally, fungal and bacterial illnesses can strike orchids, particularly under extremely wet growth circumstances. Important measures in preventing disease include having enough ventilation, not putting water on the leaves, and using fungicides when needed. It is important to put fresh orchids under quarantine to avoid bringing pests or illnesses into an already-existing collection. Orchid plants are certain to live a long and healthy life if they receive regular maintenance along with aggressive pest and disease management.

CHAPTER SEVEN

BUSINESS PLANNING FOR ORCHIDS

CREATING A BUSINESS STRATEGY

A thorough business plan is an essential first step for any corporation hoping to succeed and last. Outlining the company's mission, vision, goals, and the tactics required to attain them, this strategic document functions as a roadmap.

It entails a thorough analysis of all relevant internal and external elements, including advantages, disadvantages, opportunities, and threats. A well-written business plan serves as a communication tool for possible partners, investors, and stakeholders in addition to offering direction to the company.

The firm overview, market analysis, financial projections, and operational strategies are usually included in its sections.

MARKET RESEARCH AND ANALYSIS

The cornerstones of a successful company plan are market research and analysis. Businesses are better equipped to meet client needs by customizing their strategies and making informed decisions based on their grasp of industry trends, consumer behavior, and market dynamics. The process of collecting and analyzing data on competitors, target markets, and business possibilities is known as market research. Businesses may determine their unique value offer, gauge market demand, and improve their positioning with the help of a comprehensive investigation. This procedure promotes a proactive response to shifts in the market and consumer preferences by helping businesses identify development opportunities and potential obstacles.

PRICING TACTICS

A company's competitiveness and profitability are greatly influenced by its pricing tactics.

When developing their pricing models, businesses need to take into account several elements, including perceived customer value, rival prices, and manufacturing costs. worth-based pricing, which takes into account the perceived worth of the good or service to the client, and cost-plus pricing, which adds a markup to the production cost, are examples of common pricing techniques. Businesses can also use tiered pricing, psychological pricing, and dynamic pricing strategies to enhance their pricing structure. Finding the ideal balance guarantees that the business keeps a healthy profit margin and stays competitive.

CHANNELS FOR SALES AND DISTRIBUTION

To maximize product or service accessibility and reach target consumers, efficient sales and distribution channels are necessary. Companies need to create a sales plan that complements their positioning in the market and overall business objectives. This involves choosing the right sales channels, such as retail partnerships, e-commerce, direct sales, or a mix of these. Furthermore, creating a productive distribution network guarantees that goods are delivered to clients on schedule and under budget. Using internet platforms, distributor partnerships, and store collaborations are typical strategies for increasing market penetration. A sales and distribution strategy that is flexible and agile enables companies to react to shifts in the market and changing customer preferences.

CHAPTER EIGHT

MARKETING YOUR ORCHIDS

PACKAGING AND BRANDING

In a cutthroat industry, developing a unique brand for your orchids is crucial. Your brand should highlight the special attributes of your orchids, such as their eye-catching hues, unusual species, or superb maintenance techniques. Create a unique tagline, logo, and visual identity that captures the spirit of your orchid company. Building brand recognition requires consistency in branding across a range of platforms, including websites, social media, and packaging.

When it comes to orchid marketing, packaging is essential. Create packaging that not only shields the fragile flowers from harm but also acts as an outward manifestation of your brand. Take into account environmentally friendly packaging choices to satisfy consumers' increasing demands for sustainable operations. Include educational labels that emphasize how to take care of the orchid, its species, and any special qualities to improve the whole experience and happiness of the buyer.

TECHNIQUES FOR ONLINE AND OFFLINE MARKETING

Having a strong online presence is essential in the digital age. Create an easy-to-use website that highlights your types of orchids, offers maintenance advice, and enables online sales. Use social media to interact with your audience by posting eye-catching images, behind-the-scenes videos, and client endorsements. To expand your audience and increase website traffic, use internet advertising.

Marketing through offline means is still important, particularly in the horticultural sector. Investigate conventional advertising channels such as radio, print, and neighborhood gatherings. Form alliances with nearby companies to cross-promote your flowers. To get more exposure, visit farmers' markets and work with other merchants.

Since word-of-mouth advertising is extremely effective, ask pleased clients to tell others about their experiences and recommend your orchid company.

ENGAGING IN ORCHID SHOWS AND EVENTS

These occasions offer priceless chances to present your orchids to a specific group of enthusiasts and possible purchasers. Engage in local and national orchid exhibitions, showcasing the variety of your collection with eye-catching displays. Interact with guests by expressing your love of orchids and offering knowledgeable guidance on cultivation and maintenance.

To draw in local communities, think of holding workshops or orchid-related events. By doing this, you establish yourself as an industry expert and establish a direct line of communication with potential clients. During these occasions, provide special deals or promotions to encourage purchases and cultivate a devoted clientele. During these events, networking with other orchid enthusiasts and experts might lead to partnerships and collaborations.

DEVELOPING PARTNERSHIPS WITH FLORISTS AND GARDEN CENTERS:

To broaden your market reach, establish strategic alliances with florists and garden centers. To entice resale buyers, set up a wholesale price structure for your orchids. Give your partners training on orchid care and marketing materials so they can properly promote and sell your products. Work together to create unique arrangements or displays that highlight your orchids in eye-catching and imaginative ways.

A successful collaboration requires clear communication between garden centers and florists. Keep yourself updated about their seasonal preferences, inventory requirements, and impending specials. Provide continuing assistance, such as prompt delivery and helpful customer support.

CHAPTER NINE

BUDGETING AND FINANCIAL MANAGEMENT FOR ORCHID FARMING

A crucial component of financial management in orchid farming is budgeting, which entails scheduling and assigning funds to different tasks involved in the growing process. Preparing the ground, buying seeds, fertilizers, pesticides, personnel, equipment, and other operational costs are all included in a well-structured budget. It acts as a guide for making financial decisions, assisting growers of orchids in tracking their expenses, setting reasonable financial objectives, and allocating resources wisely during culture. A well-planned budget also helps farmers to foresee future difficulties and modify their financial plans appropriately.

PROFITABILITY AND COST ANALYSIS

In orchid farming, cost analysis and profitability evaluation are essential components of the financial management process.

To comprehend the direct and indirect costs paid during the production process, farmers must perform comprehensive cost studies. This covers both permanent costs like land leasing and equipment upkeep as well as variable costs like those associated with inputs like seeds and fertilizer. Farmers can determine their profitability margins by comparing these expenses to the money received from orchid sales. Making educated judgments, maximizing the use of available resources, and improving overall financial performance all depends on this information.

KEEPING UP WITH FINANCIAL DOCUMENTS

Maintaining accurate financial records is essential to successful financial management in orchid cultivation. An accurate and thorough accounting of revenue and outlays, including invoices and receipts, gives a clear picture of the orchid company's financial situation. More accountability, tax compliance, and improved decision-making are facilitated by well-organized financial data.

It also facilitates the creation of stronger financial strategies for sustainable orchid farming and helps identify areas where cost-cutting measures can be put into place.

GETTING GRANTS AND FUNDING

A crucial component of financial management for orchid growers aiming to grow or streamline their business is obtaining grants and funding. Having access to finance is essential for purchasing new farming equipment, buying land, and applying cutting-edge agriculture methods. Orchid farmers can look into several financial options, including subsidies from government organizations, loans for agriculture, and collaborations with private investors. A strong business plan increases the chances of successfully obtaining funding by proving the feasibility and prospective profitability of the orchid-growing endeavor.

CHAPTER TEN

OBSTACLES AND SOLUTIONS IN THE PRODUCTION OF ORCHIDS

TYPICAL OBSTACLES ORCHID FARMERS FACE

Despite being a lucrative endeavor, growing orchids can be challenging for growers. To ensure effective cultivation, creative solutions and best practices are needed. Orchid farmers often encounter the difficulty of their plants' vulnerability to illnesses and vermin. Because of their heightened sensitivity to environmental changes, orchids are particularly vulnerable to illnesses and infestations. Bacterial and fungal infections can spread fast among orchids, endangering the entire crop. In response, farmers are reducing their reliance on chemical interventions by using biopesticides, integrating natural predators, and implementing integrated pest management techniques.

Accurately controlling growing conditions is another issue in orchid farming. Species-specific requirements for temperature, humidity, and light are different for orchids. It can be difficult to maintain these ideal circumstances, particularly in large-scale operations. Technological innovations like smart sensors and automatic climate control systems are being used to address this. With the aid of these instruments, orchid producers may more precisely monitor and modify environmental factors, leading to healthier orchid growth.

CREATIVE REMEDIES AND OPTIMAL TECHNIQUES

For orchid growers, the scarcity of appropriate planting materials presents additional difficulty. Expanding orchid collections can be challenging for farmers who cultivate certain orchid species due to limited choices for propagation. A method that makes it possible to produce large numbers of orchids from small amounts of plant material is tissue culture techniques. This process guarantees the genetic purity of the orchids and solves the problem of shortage at the same time, producing consistently high-quality flowers.

The availability of markets and transportation presents other difficulties for orchid growers. Because they are fragile flowers, orchids must be handled carefully when being transported to avoid damage. Moreover, it might be difficult for small-scale farmers in particular to obtain access to lucrative markets. Farmers are now able to solve transportation difficulties as a group and bargain for better market prospects thanks to cooperative efforts and the creation of marketing networks.

A vital component of growing orchids successfully is balancing the flow of nutrients and water. Inadequate nutrition levels or excessive irrigation can cause root rot and poor flowering.

Growers are using more and more specialized nutrient formulations and precision irrigation systems to adjust their practices to the unique requirements of individual orchid varietals. This focused strategy improves overall crop health while simultaneously conserving resources.

Growing orchids poses a special set of problems that need for a fusion of conventional knowledge and creative fixes. To maintain the health and vitality of their crops, orchid growers are always evolving, whether it is through disease management or technological solutions. Orchid growers can overcome these obstacles and build successful orchid enterprises by adhering to best practices and staying abreast of industry changes.